CW01476008

GIBRALTAR JOURNAL

Nº 1   A GLORIOUS GALLOP THROUGH THE HISTORY OF GIBRALTAR   FIRST EDITION

ROCK'S PREHISTORIC VISITORS

ARCHAEOLOGICAL DIG UNEARTHS RELICS OF ANCIENT HUMANS

BY OUR CULTURE EDITOR
2 September 2014

LABYRINTHINE CAVES IN Gibraltar have revealed a work of cave art from humanity's distant past. But even more remarkable is that archaeologists led by Professor Clive Finlayson, director of the Gibraltar Museum, yesterday published claims that the pattern of etched lines was inscribed not by our own species, *Homo sapiens*, but by a different ancient people – *Homo neanderthalensis*.

The markings were found in the Gorham's Cave Complex that honeycombs the Rock, once kilometres from the shore but now just a few metres above the waves. There are more than 210 caves in the Rock, carved over hundreds of thousands of years by water seeping through the limestone formation.

The artwork is made up of lines in a grid pattern scratched deep into rock at an intersection in the caves. The layers of sediment overlying the artwork contains stone tools made in the same style as those used by Neanderthals throughout Europe, indicating the people who made the artwork were probably Neanderthals themselves.

Archaeologists using replicas of stone tools from the period found that in order to make such deep cuts, the tools had to be passed repeatedly through grooves in the tough dolomite rock hundreds of times. This would have taken at least an hour and must have been a deliberate act to create the precise pattern. It was once thought Neanderthals were brutish and primitive but recent finds including these suggest they created art, played musical instruments and buried their dead.

Neanderthals are believed to have arrived in the caves around 125,000 years ago. The labyrinth is also thought to have been their last refuge as recently as just 32,000 years ago. They then disappeared, possibly due to a combination of climate change and competition with *Homo sapiens*. However, recent research shows Neanderthal DNA in almost all modern people of Eurasian background, suggesting they lived together and even interbred for thousands of years. Professor Finlayson says the latest find 'brings the Neanderthals closer to us yet again'.

Following the Neanderthals' disappearance, modern humans moved into the caves and left decorated axes and paintings of red deer.

The Rock emerged from below the waves as the continents of Europe and Africa collided 20 million years ago. As the mountain was thrust upwards it started to tilt, a process continuing ever since. The Mediterranean basin has dried out and flooded several times as the converging continents first separated it from the Atlantic Ocean and then sea levels rose and fell, filling up the basin for the last time around 5 million years ago.

New trade port established near Gibraltar

MERCHANTS AND traders exploring the vast, mysterious and treacherous Atlantic Ocean have announced the founding of a new city situated on the Bay of Gibraltar. The new port will be an essential staging post for trading voyages through the nearby Strait of Gibraltar. The Strait was once considered the end of the world, but is now known to connect the Mediterranean Sea with the Atlantic, *reports our business editor in 800 BC.*

The traders hail from Tyre, a Phoenician city at the eastern end of the Mediterranean Sea, every corner of which is now part of their trading network. Phoenician vessels, the most seaworthy yet built, have ventured into the dangerous waters of the Atlantic, bringing back ivory from the west coast of Africa and tin, used with copper to make the tough and valuable metal alloy bronze, from the distant northern island of Britain.

GREEKS IDENTIFY ROCK AS ONE OF 'PILLARS OF HERCULES'

BY OUR CULTURE EDITOR
460 BC

GEOGRAPHERS, POETS and other scholars from Greece have developed a new theory for the formation of the Strait of Gibraltar, identifying the demigod Hercules as its creator.

The Greek scholars suggest that the demigod split what was once a solid mountain down the middle, allowing the waters of the Atlantic Ocean to flood in. They have taken to calling the two mountains, which they know as Calpe (the Rock of Gibraltar) and Abila (Jebel Musa in North Africa), the 'Pillars of Hercules'.

Hercules is thought to have visited the location as he performed the 10th of his 12 exhausting labours – to take the giant cattle of the monster-king Geryon from his home near Gibraltar. The Greeks are not the first to associate the Rock with the gods: Phoenician sailors would leave offerings of jewellery, ceramics and expensive perfumes in caves on the eastern shore of the Rock, asking for divine protection for their voyages into the dangers of the Atlantic.

ROMANS SET SIGHTS ON GIBRALTAR

BY OUR WAR CORRESPONDENT
206 BC

THE WAR BETWEEN THE Roman Republic and its rivals, the Carthaginian Empire, has seen a decisive sea and land battle for control of the Iberian Peninsula. A small Roman fleet under Gaius Laelius routed Carthaginian forces controlling the Bay of Gibraltar, the key strategic location in the struggle between the superpowers for the control of the Mediterranean.

Laelius had been plotting with Carthaginians sympathetic to Rome in the port-city of Carteia. But hopes of a bloodless takeover were scuppered when he intercepted an enemy ship carrying the captured conspirators on their way to the centre of Carthage's empire to face punishment. Their plot had been discovered!

The Romans turned the situation to their advantage with an attack by land and sea. Despite the strength of Carthage's fleet and their sea-prowess, the Roman fleet of seven triremes and one quinquereme was too strong for them. The presence of Laelius's quinquereme flagship with five banks of oars, rather than the three of a trireme, was decisive and it defeated three enemy ships. Rowed by hundreds of oarsmen, the Roman warships carry crack troops to storm enemy vessels and land positions, and are equipped with rams to sink ships.

Mela puts Gibraltar on the map

A landmark description of world geography has been published by Gibraltar local Pomponius Mela, writes our science editor in AD 43. *He describes the Rock of Gibraltar as sparsely populated, due to poor soil and the scarcity of water, as well as filled with wide-chambered caves.*

Mela's revolutionary theories divide the world into five regions – two frozen poles and a central, hot, impassable desert. To the north and south of this are temperate, inhabited areas including the Mediterranean. De situ orbis, 'On the place of the world', is the first dedicated geography in Latin.

VISIGOTHS DECLARE NEW KINGDOM IN HISPANIA

MARAUDING WARRIOR tribes, called the Visigoths, yesterday announced the founding of a new kingdom in Iberia stretching from southern France down to the Strait of Gibraltar, *writes our political editor in AD 507.*

The Visigoths have fled climate change and war in their native Germany, fighting their way through Europe in search of a new homeland. Their migration is one of many in the power vacuum left by the collapse of the Roman Empire, whose army is now stretched too thin to protect all its territories.

The Visigoths are followers of Arius who teaches that God created Christ, rather than Christ being one element in the 'Trinity'. This dispute is bound to aggravate conflict with the Visigoth's Catholic neighbours in their newly founded kingdom.

MOORISH INVASION

NORTH-AFRICAN GENERAL TARIQ REVEALS PLANS TO CONTINUE EUROPEAN CONQUEST

BY OUR WAR CORRESPONDENT
30 April AD 711

THE ISLAMIC CALIPHATE arrived in Europe yesterday sending shockwaves through Christendom, with the troops of general Tariq ibn Ziyad crossing the Strait of Gibraltar and occupying the Rock. The audacious attack is the first attempt by the Islamic religious revolution to expand into western Europe after its dramatic sweep through North Africa from the Arabian Peninsula.

Tariq, a North African, serves the Emir of Ifriqiyah. The invasion was assisted by Julian, Count of Ceuta, who opposes the tyrannical Roderic, King of the Visigoths.

Moorish raids began last year when a small band led by Tarif abu Zarah attacked and looted the port of Julia Traducta, quickly returning to North Africa with booty and prisoners. Tarif's followers have renamed the port-town 'Tarifa' in his honour.

By hiding his army of 7,000 Berber cavalrymen on ships provided by his ally Julian, Tariq's attack took the Visigoths by surprise. The vessels looked like many on trading voyages from the Mediterranean to the Atlantic. Instead of attacking Tarifa like his predecessor, he made for the poorly defended Rock of Gibraltar. Tariq was careful to stay out of sight of the Visigoth commander at Algeciras and landed his force in secret at night to quickly take the Rock with little resistance.

Muslim rule has spread rapidly from Arabia across North Africa over the previous century. Moorish sources suggest that yesterday's attack marks the beginning of a sustained Islamic campaign in Iberia. For the moment Tariq's landing at the Rock (which his soldiers have taken to calling Jabal Tariq, meaning 'mountain of Tariq', after their leader) has gone smoothly, but a major battle with Visigoth forces seems inevitable in the near future – a battle to decide the fate of the fractured kingdom of the Visigoths and possibly of all Christianity in Iberia.

Bold building programme continues

A NEW BATHHOUSE, OR hammam in Arabic, was opened yesterday, the latest in the transformative series of new buildings and fortifications constructed at Gibraltar by the Rock's Moorish rulers. Once a neglected outpost of Christian Hispania, the peninsula of Gibraltar has been developed into a bustling fortress and cultural centre at the heart of Moorish power in the western Mediterranean, writes our culture editor in 1350.

As soon as they arrived, Moorish leaders began setting up the first permanent settlement on the Rock – the fortified 'Medina al-Fath' or 'City of Victory', with three sets of walls, a castle and palaces. The fortress ensures the key strategic location remains in the hands of the Moors.

However, the new private bathhouse is strictly recreational and uses the Roman hypocaust system for heating, advanced technology largely forgotten in Christian Europe. The floor is raised on pillars. Hot air, heated by a furnace, is circulated under it and through hollow walls of the pool and surrounding rooms with different temperatures.

Hygiene plays an important part in Islamic philosophy. Many Muslims believe prayer should only be undertaken when the proper rituals of cleansing have been observed. Hygiene is also a key element in Islamic medicine, which is far more developed than neighbouring Christian societies, and includes the provision of hospitals and healthcare to all parts of society, rich or poor.

SIEGE SEES SPANISH TAKE CONTROL

750 YEARS OF MOORISH Gibraltar finally ended yesterday with the surrender of the fortress to Christian forces. Its Moorish and Jewish inhabitants have been driven from their homes and forced to leave the city, *reports our war correspondent on 21 August 1462*.

Gibraltar has suffered eight sieges as the Christian Kingdom of Castile and Muslim powers fought for control, control that until yesterday had almost constantly been in the hands of the Moors.

Plans were drawn up for the siege after a Moorish convert to Christianity revealed to the governor of Tarifa that Gibraltar was poorly defended. The governor called for support from nearby Christian towns, including Medina-Sidonia, and set about besieging the city. The lord of Medina-Sidonia, Juan Alonso de Guzmán, had a personal interest in attacking the fortress – his own father had been killed in the previous attempt to take it 25 years earlier, and was subsequently mutilated and his body parts hung from a basket above the walls as a warning to other attackers.

The conquest is the latest chapter in the ongoing *Reconquista*, the Spanish war to take the Moorish kingdoms of Iberia for Christianity. Moorish forces fear that the loss of Gibraltar, their first foothold in Hispania, heralds the the end of Moorish Andalusia.

Conquering couple declare Reconquista *over*

THE LAST BASTION OF Muslim Iberia, the city of Granada, has fallen to the Spanish Christian monarchs Isabel and Ferdinand, reports our political editor on 3 January 1492. The surrender ends the centuries-long war of the Reconquista.

Moorish rule in Spain had expanded since their first arrival in AD 711 under General Tariq, and at one time their dominion reached as far as the French border. But today Isabel and Ferdinand's Christian kingdom stretches all the way from the Pyrenees in the north to the Strait of Gibraltar in the south. Across the Strait, Moorish rule continues in North Africa.

As Queen of Castile, Isabel is among the most powerful Spanish rulers. Upon her marriage to Ferdinand, King of Aragon, Christian power in Spain was consolidated for the first time in the hands of a joint Christian force. The relationship has allowed them to achieve what Christian rulers in Spain have attempted for so long: to put an end to Moorish power in the peninsula.

But Isabel and Ferdinand have also been driven by religious fervour and founded the Spanish Inquisition in 1478 to impose strict Catholic Christianity – rumours are spreading that they plan to convert or exile all non-Christians from Spain, including large Muslim and Jewish populations in locations such as Gibraltar.

CORSAIRS RAVAGE ROCK

BY OUR WAR CORRESPONDENT
11 September 1540

BARBARY CORSAIRS mounted a devastating attack on Gibraltar yesterday. Turkish and Moorish fleets, which frequently terrorise the Mediterranean, pillaged and looted the settlement on the Rock, making off with wealth as well as hundreds of captives as hostages or to sell into slavery.

The corsairs, licensed to attack Christians by the Islamic Ottoman Empire, seize ships in the Mediterranean and Atlantic, while residents of coastal settlements as far away as Britain and Iceland live in constant fear of their raids. The attack on Gibraltar was organised by the most notorious of the corsairs – Barbarossa, 'Red-beard' in Italian, who is based in Algiers in North Africa. He had help in planning the raid from a turncoat named Caramani, who had escaped from the penal settlement on the Rock and fled to North Africa with dreams of returning to Gibraltar to loot it.

Thousands of corsairs came ashore at Europa Point last night taking defenders by complete surprise. While the tiny garrison cowered helplessly behind the castle walls, the attackers looted homes and ships at anchor before making off with captives. Those with wealthy families or friends were destined to be ransomed while the rest would end their days in slavery.

However, the arrival of a Spanish fleet signalled a change in the fortunes of both the corsairs and their captives. In the ensuing naval clash, many of the Barbary ships were captured and many prisoners freed and returned to Gibraltar, others were swapped for corsairs captured in the battle.

Yesterday's tragic events highlight the neglect of the fortress and other defences at Gibraltar since the Spanish takeover. The fortifications are in dire need of improvement along with the establishment of a naval base to repel future invaders such as the corsairs, but Spanish rulers have shown little interest in the strategically important peninsula.

ANGLO–DUTCH FLEET TAKES THE ROCK

BUT *JOURNAL* ASKS 'ARE NEW OCCUPIERS HERE TO STAY?'

BY OUR WAR CORRESPONDENT
4 August 1704

G IBRALTAR HAS BEEN seized in a daring naval assault by Anglo–Dutch forces, beginning a new chapter in its history. The peninsula, in Spanish hands for 240 years, surrendered this morning under cannon fire from ships and an assault by thousands of marines and sailors.

The attack was ordered by English Admiral Sir George Rooke and German Prince George of Hesse-Darmstadt, commanding the Dutch forces. Rooke's mission was to attack the port of Cadiz but the admiral had turned his attention to Gibraltar because of its strategic value and small garrison.

On 1 August, Prince George landed forces on the isthmus to the north of the Rock and sent a letter to the Spanish governor Don Diego de Salinas requesting the city's surrender. Despite his hopeless position, Don Diego gallantly refused.

The next morning, Rooke began to bombard the city and its fortifications from the sea in preparation for a full-scale assault. Dutch forces attacked from the isthmus while English marines landed at the opposite side of the city, trapping the garrison.

Two captains, William Jumper and Jasper Hicks, saw the New Mole, a fortified harbour wall, was undefended and, acting perhaps recklessly and apparently without orders, stormed ashore with their men. Their daring assault was cut short when a Spanish gunpowder magazine exploded, killing 42 and wounding many others, including Captain Hicks. Despite this calamity, the harbour was secured by English reinforcements under the command of Captain Edward Whitaker. The English have already renamed the spot 'Jumper's Bastion'.

The Spanish governor Don Diego de Salinas called a ceasefire and his surrender was accepted by Prince George, who ensured the garrison's right to leave in safety.

The victory is part of the 'War of the Spanish Succession', a conflict about who rules Spain, which has ignited a powder keg of long-standing rivalries between countries across Europe. Whether the allies intend to maintain control of the Rock after the war is over remains to be seen.

TREATY MAKES GIBRALTAR BRITISH 'IN PERPETUITY'

P EACE HAS FINALLY come to Europe with the continent's leaders signing the Treaty of Utrecht, ending the 13-year-long 'War of the Spanish Succession', *writes our political correspondent on 13 July 1713.*

Article X of the treaty, named after the Dutch city where it was agreed, grants control of Gibraltar to Britain 'for ever, without any exception or impediment whatsoever'. However, it also contains clauses continuing Spanish policies governing the Rock, including barring its use for smuggling and, controversially, banning Moors and Jews from living there.

Even more grievous for the pride of Spain than the loss of Gibraltar is the division of its huge empire. However, King Philip V has at last won recognition as rightful ruler of Spain from the major powers of Europe, including Queen Anne of the now-unified Kingdom of Great Britain and Ireland.

SIEGE TO END ALL SIEGES GRIPS GIB
SPANISH SURROUND ROCK BUT ELIOTT STANDS FIRM

BY OUR WAR CORRESPONDENT
20 June 1779

SPANISH AND FRENCH forces today began a total blockade of Gibraltar, determined to recapture the city from the British. Defenders and civilian residents of Gibraltar have braced themselves for a long and gruelling siege.

The UK has found itself catapulted into another European war with France and Spain as the two nations step in to exploit the rebellion by many of Britain's colonies in America. They also want to reclaim lost territory, including Gibraltar, an essential step towards breaking British naval superiority in both the Mediterranean and the Atlantic as a prelude to invading the British Isles themselves.

Previous land attacks on Gibraltar have led to heavy casualties. It is thought the plan is now for a long siege rather than a

costly assault. Spanish fleets at Algeciras and Ceuta are preventing any attempts to resupply the garrison by sea, and Spain's leaders have persuaded Morocco, which has often traded with Gibraltar in times of crisis, not to try to break the blockade.

But the besieging forces may find the Rock's defenders stronger willed than they expect – especially under the leadership of new Governor-General Sir George Augustus Eliott. The general is known to be tough and holds the 5,382 men under his command to

his high expectations. Eliott refuses both meat and alcohol, sleeps little, and has great experience, having served on many battlefields and been wounded many times. While Eliott's men are well supplied with shot and powder, they have very limited stocks of winter fuel, fresh food and water.

British lookouts say the besieging forces are constructing forts, trenches and gun emplacements opposite defences, and will soon begin a sustained bombardment of the city, intended to break the garrison's morale and encourage them to surrender. The city is expected to suffer greatly at the hands of the Spanish artillery and many civilians are leaving the Rock aboard the few ships which have been able to make it past the blockade.

But Eliott has no intention of surrendering the key location to Spain, and his forces continue to wait anxiously for news of relief or reinforcement from Britain.

ENGINEERS BEGIN BLASTING ROCK
TUNNELS MAY BREAK SIEGE, SAYS ELIOTT

BY OUR WAR CORRESPONDENT
25 May 1782

BRITISH DEFENDERS ARE turning to unusual measures to break the Great Siege of Gibraltar as it approaches its third year. Today, soldiers began mining tunnels, digging and blasting through the Rock to create new gun emplacements to fire on the Spanish forces below.

The tunnels are the brain-child of Henry Ince, Methodist preacher, former miner and Sergeant-Major of the Soldier Artificer Company. They will allow Governor Eliott to establish an elevated gun battery

deploying a new type of cannon that can fire downwards at the besieging enemy without being damaged by recoil. Developed by Royal Artillery Lieutenant George Koehler it can also be swung sideways to be level for reloading without exposing gunners to enemy fire.

Some enemy guns were destroyed in an audacious raid last year, but the garrison and civilian population are exhausted by constant bombardment and the depredations of scurvy and smallpox, while much of the city now lies in ruins.

Word has reached British forces that powerful enemy warships are being developed specifically for a major attack on Gibraltar. Eliott has authorised the use of 'hot potatoes', cannonballs heated until red-hot, which he hopes will set the ships ablaze before they can open fire. The worst of the siege may be yet to come.

Gib's great siege comes to an end

THE LONGEST SIEGE IN British military history has finally come to an end, reports our war correspondent on 10 March 1783. *Spanish leaders have withdrawn their disheartened forces from the siege works and informed Gibraltar's exhausted defenders that a peace has been agreed between Britain and Spain after three years and seven months.*

For centuries, the history of the strategic Rock has been dominated by conflict as factions vie for control, the 5th siege even claiming the life of Castilian King Alfonso XI in 1350. Today's ceasefire marks the end of the 14th siege at Gibraltar.

The garrison's unyielding defence of the Rock has today ensured Britain's continuing control of Gibraltar, a key naval base for its domination of the seas.

SHOCK BATTLE AT TRAFALGAR

VICE-ADMIRAL NELSON KILLED IN THE CONFLICT, BUT NAPOLEON'S PLANS TO INVADE BRITAIN SCUPPERED

BY OUR WAR CORRESPONDENT
28 October 1805

THE BATTERED BRITISH SHIPS that crushed Napoleon's French and Spanish fleet off Cape Trafalgar in southern Spain have finally limped into Gibraltar nearly a week after the decisive battle.

However, victory came at the cost of England's dearest blood with British sailors mourning the loss of their revered commander, Vice-Admiral Lord Nelson, along with another 457 of their shipmates. French and Spanish losses were far higher, with 3,233 killed in battle and another 3,000 believed drowned in the storm that followed.

Nelson had been patrolling the Strait, hunting for the enemy ships commanded by French Admiral Pierre de Villeneuve, which had been criss-crossing the Mediterranean to evade the British Royal Navy.

In a typically brilliant and unorthodox move, Nelson had divided his fleet into two columns and attacked the French and Spanish from the side. The surprised enemy was smashed into three disorganised groups, which were then torn to pieces by the British warships.

The Admiral, standing on deck refusing to cover his many conspicuous medals, was shot by a sharpshooter from the rigging of a French warship. Surgeons were unable to save him from the wound that pierced his shoulder, lung and spine and he died three hours later, but only after hearing victory was certain.

Horatio Nelson's dismasted and crippled flagship, the 104-gun HMS *Victory*, now lies in Gibraltar harbour. On board, his body is preserved in a barrel of brandy, guarded by his devoted sailors.

HMS *Victory* had visited Gibraltar before, at the head of a relief fleet during the Great Siege at the end of the last century. Now her crew work feverishly to make repairs so they can have the honour of taking Nelson's body home to England for a hero's funeral.

If Napoleon's fleet reached the English Channel they would have carried his army to invade Britain – an attack seen as almost certain since 1803 but, thanks to victory at Trafalgar, that will now never happen. Napoleon's defeat ends his dreams of world domination. Isolated in Europe, he faces a British Empire determined to free the continent from his tyranny.

PICKLE RACES TO BRITAIN WITH NEWS OF BATTLE

NEWS OF A MOMENTOUS NAVAL BATTLE two weeks ago at Trafalgar has reached England aboard a small British ship landing at Falmouth in Cornwall, reports our war correspondent on 4 November 1805.

The vessel, HMS Pickle, set off nine days ago from Gibraltar with reports not only of victory but also the death of Admiral Lord Nelson, first published in the Gibraltar Chronicle *on 24 October 1805.*

As Pickle, a fast but small and lightly armed schooner, raced to Britain, its captain, John Lapenotière, threw its guns overboard to lighten the ship in order to deliver its fateful news as soon as possible.

Having arrived at Falmouth, the captain immediately took a fast carriage to London.

'100-Ton Gun' watches over Strait

THE FIRST OF TWO enormous state-of-the-art guns capable of hitting a target eight miles away arrived today at Gibraltar. With that range they could shoot across the Strait to Africa, giving Gibraltar and Britain control of the entrance to the Mediterranean, writes our war correspondent on 19 December 1882.

The weapons, firing shells weighing 2,000 pounds each, are named '100-ton guns' after their weight. They are thought to be the largest and, at a cost of £16,000 each, the most expensive guns ever made. High-tech steam power is used to load and aim. The boilers must be kept at full steam or need several hours to warm up before the guns can be used.

Initial testing of the weapon at Gibraltar came to a halt when a shell became stuck in the barrel. A brave volunteer agreed to climb in and free the shell, which might have fired at any moment. He was immediately promoted.

Two identical weapons have also been supplied to the garrison on Malta, south of Italy. The four guns amplify Britain's presence in the Mediterranean and help secure the new direct route to India and China through the Suez Canal.

MYSTERY ABOARD MARY CELESTE

BY OUR CRIME CORRESPONDENT
23 January 1873

A BRITISH COURT inquiry in Gibraltar today finished its investigation of the mysterious disappearance of all ten souls aboard the sailing vessel *Mary Celeste*. The Salvage Court sitting in Gibraltar reported yesterday to the London Board of Trade with suspicions of foul play but no explanation of how the American brigantine was left drifting off the Azores.

None of the eight-man crew, its captain Benjamin Brigg, nor his wife and young daughter, aboard when the ship left New York, have been found. The *Mary Celeste* was spotted on December the 5th by another merchant vessel, the *Dei Gratia*, sailing erratically with its sails in disarray some 600 miles from Gibraltar. Realising the vessel was in trouble, *Dei Gratia*'s Captain Morehouse sent two crew members to investigate.

They were shocked to find no one aboard, but saw little obvious cause for the ship's abandonment. Some nautical documents and instruments, along with the ship's boat, were missing. The last log was dated 10 days previously. *Mary Celeste*'s cargo of industrial alcohol lay undisturbed. Captain Morehouse ordered four of his crew to take command of *Mary Celeste* and sail to Gibraltar.

The Inquiry's British prosecutor Frederick Solly-Flood presented theories that the missing were murdered by the crew of the *Dei Gratia* for the salvage fee, or the captain's family were murdered by his own drunken crew, or even that the crew had been killed by strangely unavaricious pirates.

However, more obvious explanations have been put forward, such as that the crew abandoned ship to escape its perceived imminent destruction from freak weather leaving it in chaos, or because of intolerable and explosive fumes released from the cargo. The tragic loss of the ship's crew is a mystery that may never be solved.

WAR OVER AT LAST, BUT BRITANNIA SUNK

THE GREAT WAR THAT has engulfed Europe ended this morning, but in Gibraltar, celebrations are muted by the tragic sinking of the battleship HMS *Britannia* just two days ago, *writes our war correspondent on 11 November 1918.* The 50 men killed were among the very last victims of the war.

Britannia was torpedoed by a German submarine off Cape Trafalgar near the Atlantic entrance to the Strait. She lost power and sank three hours later. Most casualties were caused by toxic smoke. While the rest of the world celebrates the end of the war, today sees Gibraltar holding the memorial service for *Britannia*'s dead.

The armistice, an agreement to cease hostilities, was signed this morning between the allied powers – Britain, France, the USA and Russia – and their German foes, coming into effect at 11am, to end one of the bloodiest wars in history. The Great War saw fighting across the globe that led to the deaths of at least 15 million people. Now leaders of all nations promise such a war must never happen again.

LAST VOYAGE OF THE MONS CALPE

AS LIFELINE VESSEL DEPARTS THE ROCK FOR FINAL TIME, THE *JOURNAL* LOOKS BACK AT 40 YEARS OF CHANGE AT GIBRALTAR

BY OUR CULTURE EDITOR
1986

MONS CALPE, THE much-loved Gibraltar ferry, began its final voyage from the Rock today, embarking on a new career as she began the trip to her next home in Cyprus. The ship will be renamed *City of Limassol*, after her new home port.

The passenger and vehicle ferry became Gibraltar's precious lifeline when the frontier with Spain was closed for 16 years from 1969. Apart from planes and passing ships, she was the only source of supplies and the only access to the outside world for the Rock's residents. The blockade was fully lifted last year and the vessel has been sold off, now unable to compete with ferries from Algeciras just over the frontier.

The ship could hold 580 passengers and 80 cars and was built in 1954 for Bland's Gibraltar to Tangier line, Mons Calpe being the Roman name for the Rock.

Forty-two years in service saw many changes in the ferry's home port. Gibraltar has recovered from the war and her evacuated civilian population has returned with a unique Gibraltarian identity. The Rock itself has steadily changed from a military outpost to a Crown Colony and then finally to a self-governing dependent territory in 1981, its people enjoying the status of British citizens. Friction with Spain over ownership peaked that same year when honeymooning Charles and Diana sailed out of the harbour on HMY *Britannia*. It is rumoured the Queen responded to the furious Spanish King Juan Carlos with 'My yacht, my son, my Rock.' The following year the frontier was reopened, and relations have begun to cool.

Today the House of Assembly, Gibraltar's parliament, sits in the old Exchange and Commercial Library, built by merchants in 1817 and used to discuss important civilian matters ever since. The ownership dispute with Spain continues to dominate the Rock's politics, with concern at both Spain and Britain's future intentions for sovereignty.

JOINT SOVEREIGNTY WITH SPAIN REJECTED IN REFERENDUM

A RADICAL PLAN TO share sovereignty of Gibraltar between Britain and Spain has been thrown out by the Rock's residents. In a referendum yesterday almost 99% of Gibraltarian voters rejected the proposal, *our political correspondent reports on 8 November 2002.*

Initial talks were held between Britain and Spain last year without the knowledge of the government of Gibraltar, which organised the referendum, the second in 35 years, when they finally heard of the plan. Although the British Foreign Office has refused to recognise the result, it is likely to kill the joint sovereignty proposal for the foreseeable future. It has also damaged the people of Gibraltar's trust in the London government, but not their determination to remain British.

The Foreign Office has been criticised for planning Gibraltar's future without consulting its people, as is guaranteed in the constitution should the political status of the Rock look likely to change. Spain also rejected the referendum results calling it 'illegal'.

As Gibraltar enters a new century, the issue of its sovereignty looks unlikely to be resolved any time soon.

UK votes to leave EU – but Gib disagrees

THE SURPRISE DECISION yesterday that Britain will leave the European Union has sent shockwaves through Gibraltar, which had a higher vote to remain than any other part of Britain, writes our political correspondent on 24 June 2016.

The referendum across the UK was close with 48% voting to remain and 52% to leave. However, in Gibraltar 96% voted to stay. Gibraltar's economy is heavily reliant on an open frontier with Spain allowing access for workers, goods and services. It is feared leaving the EU may again end free movement, endangering Gibraltar's right to self-determination. Furthermore, Britain's exit from the EU may encourage Spain to make more concerted efforts to claim Gibraltar.

Now Britain's politicians must begin the difficult task, lasting at least two years, of preparing for the long road to Brexit and a new future for the country, one Gibraltarians are determined should include them.

UNESCO RECOGNISES GIB'S PAST

NEW CABLE CAR PLANNED FOR ROCK'S FUTURE

GIBRALTAR

BY OUR CULTURE EDITOR
10 July 2016

THE UNIQUE STORY OF Gibraltar's prehistoric past has been recognised by it being inscribed as a World Heritage Site by UNESCO, the United Nations' body supporting education, science and culture.

The move is intended to promote the artefacts and sites from 100,000 years of humans living on the Rock. The oldest finds come from the Gorham's Cave Complex – the vast web of caves opening up from the eastern shore. Discoveries include ancient artwork and bird bones left by early humans called Neanderthals. Sophisticated stone tools by our own species Homo sapiens have also been recovered. The cave complex may represent the last home of the Neanderthals, as their populations gradually declined about 32,000 years ago, seemingly displaced by Homo sapiens elsewhere in Europe.

Visitors today can reach the top of the Rock itself by cable car, due to undergo a major refurbishment in the very-near future. This gives access to the magnificent views in all directions from the Upper Rock Nature Reserve and to the newly opened suspension bridge soaring over a 50-metre gorge. Visitors can also reach the Mediterranean Steps from here, although the UNESCO site is off-limits without special permission.

A unique history runs through Gibraltar, like the caves through the Rock itself. As Gibraltar moves into the 21st century, it continues to look with pride on its past and optimism towards its future, confident in overcoming the challenges ahead by the same resourceful and resilient character that Gibraltarians have demonstrated throughout their history.

UNFOLD THE TIMELINE HERE 👉

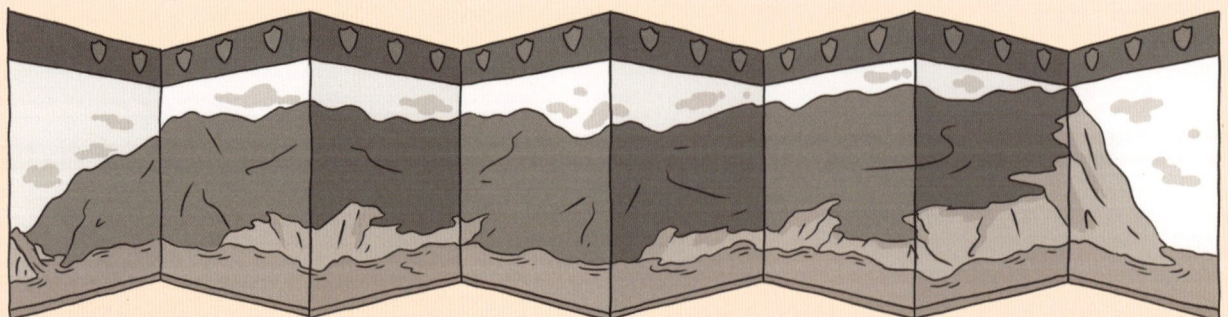

Written by **Patrick Skipworth** and **Christopher Lloyd**. Designed by **Assunção Sampayo**.
Published by What on Earth Publishing Ltd, The Black Barn, Wickhurst Farm, Leigh, Tonbridge, Kent TN11 8PS, United Kingdom.
First published in the United Kingdom in 2017. Copyright © 2017. All rights reserved.
Contact us at **info@whatonearthbooks.com** or visit **whatonearthbooks.com**

CIVIL WAR RAGES ACROSS BORDER

REFUGEES STREAM INTO GIBRALTAR AS FIERCE FIGHTING CONTINUES ALL OVER SPAIN

BY OUR WAR CORRESPONDENT
30 December 1938

SPAIN'S BRUTAL CIVIL war has spilled over into Gibraltar with a brief but ferocious naval battle in full view of the colony's shocked residents.

The Republican destroyer *José Luis Díaz* had been sheltering in the harbour with the support of local people, despite the British government's official neutrality. But when the warship slipped into the darkness last night she was greeted by the glare of flares and searchlights, instantly followed by the flash and boom of naval gunfire as she was engaged at close range by Nationalist vessels. Completely overwhelmed, she was driven onto the shore of Gibraltar's Catalan Bay to avoid being captured or sunk.

For two years General Franco's right-wing Nationalists, actively supported by fascist Germany and Italy, have been battling to wrestle control of Spain from the legitimate if controversial leftist Republican government. The Republicans seemingly have the sympathy of everyone else from communist Russia to capitalist America.

Gibraltar became involved in July 1936, when violence at the annual La Línea fair just over the frontier inside Spain forced thousands of families with children to flee in terror. Over the next few days, Spanish refugees and returning Gibraltarians streamed over the frontier on foot and by boat. The Rock's fire service entered Spain to help. Refugees were housed in spare rooms, garages and encampments on the beaches, while casualties filled Gibraltar's hospitals.

Some refugees have just crossed the frontier but others have made perilous journeys across war-torn Spain bringing stories of atrocities on both sides, but particularly by the Nationalists and German forces fighting alongside them. German aircraft are reportedly bombing and machine-gunning civilians indiscriminately, and last year destroyed the city of Guernica. There are now so many refugees that the *Gibraltar Chronicle* has begun printing in English and Spanish.

It is believed the Nationalists are steadily gaining ground, largely due to training and air support provided by Italy and Germany. However, idealists from across the globe, including Gibraltar and Britain, are fighting for Republican Spain against the Nationalists they see as tyrannical and undemocratic. It has become a clash between the century's ideologies of left and right, and also the far right and Western democracies. Many fear it will lead to a new world war.

Gibraltar remains a sanctuary for those affected by the conflict, a conflict which looks set to have serious repercussions for the Rock for decades to come.

Museum opens showcasing Gib's treasures

THE GIBRALTAR MUSEUM was opened today by the city's Governor Sir Alexander Godley, at last providing a fitting showcase for the Rock's remarkable history, writes our culture editor on 24 July 1930. The institution is the result of over a century of campaigning by local historical societies.

In the absence of a museum on the Rock, important artefacts and collections from the colony had either been lost or, like the Neanderthal skull discovered on the Rock in 1848, sent to London. Among the most unusual exhibits is an Egyptian mummy found floating in the bay by local fishermen earlier this year. Mummies are human bodies preserved for thousands of years by ancient civilisations using special techniques.

Two military buildings were donated to house the museum after they were found to be built over an amazing Moorish bathhouse, the remains of which will feature in the museum in testimony to another major period of Gibraltar's past.

Plans to boost the colony as a holiday destination and a stop-off on longer voyages include a 'Tourist Bureau', which will allow visitors to more easily see Gibraltar's incredible sights.

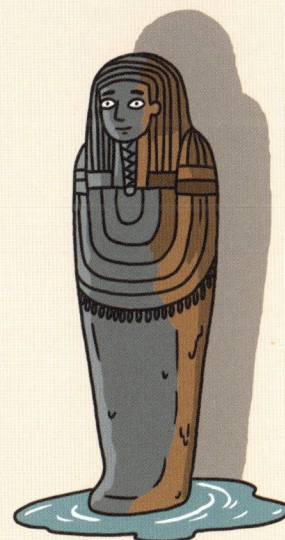

1 September 1942.
Memorandum to Commander Ian Fleming
RNVR, Room 39, Naval Intelligence
Division, The Admiralty, London.

Sir, I can report preparations
for Operation Tracer to continue
Britain's Naval Intelligence
operations from Gibraltar
should it fall are complete. I
can guarantee that in such a
calamitous event the enemy will be
completely unaware that a British
team is hidden away inside the
Rock to spy on shipping using the
harbour and Strait.

The actual chamber within the
Rock for our brave operatives
is 45 feet long and 16 feet wide
and contains provisions and
equipment needed for a six-person
team to live and operate for seven
years. There are passages from the
main chamber to hidden observation
points from the east and west
sides, allowing agents to observe
and report enemy movements, as
well as offering fresh air! Power
for the radios and ventilation
is supplied by a modified bicycle
that generates electricity while
giving the team the chance to take
exercise. Modesty aside, my special
radio apparatus works perfectly,
transmissions being received
by our Y stations in England
but completely untraceable in
Gibraltar.

Six volunteers - three radio
operatives, two doctors and an
officer in charge - have been
selected for their ability to get
on together, possibly cooped up in
Tracer for years. After training
in Kent they are now undercover in
Gibraltar, ready to be sealed up
in the 'stay-behind cave' should a
Nazi invasion occur and succeed.

I now have hope Tracer may never
be needed. Franco still rejects
Hitler's attempts to attack the
Rock through Spain, and Italian
losses in North Africa have seen
the Axis losing their Mediterranean
foothold.

Yours sincerely,

R Gambier-Parry

Col. R. Gambier-Parry MI6.

GIBRALTAR BECOMES FORTRESS AS WAR

RESIDENTS EVACUATED AS HARBOUR AND TU

BY OUR WAR CORRESPONDENT
21 May 1940

THE MASS EVACUATION OF Gibraltarian civilians began in earnest today as the war between the Allied and Axis powers escalates uncontrollably. Soon Gibraltar will be populated only by the military and a few civilians considered essential for the war effort.

Evacuees left for French-controlled Morocco packed onto the Bland Line passenger ship *Gibel Dersa*. They face an uncertain future since, if France surrenders as seems inevitable, they will have to move again. Of particular concern is the safety of Jewish Gibraltarians, due to the increasingly harsh treatment of Jewish people in Nazi-occupied Europe.

Britain is evacuating children from its cities and hopes to find refuge for up to 10,000 Gibraltarians in London. The government is looking further afield for as many as 6,000 other displaced residents. Two suggestions are the Portuguese island of Madeira, which has long-standing connections with Gibraltar, and Jamaica in the Caribbean. The latter has accommodation set up for the people of Malta, the Mediterranean island protecting the route through the Suez Canal to India and challenging Axis access to North Africa. However, Malta's civilians have refused to leave their island, insisting they will stay to fight. Gibraltar is tiny in comparison and unable to house both its people and a large wartime garrison.

The Rock has been preparing for this challenge for years, as the growing threat of the Axis powers – Germany, Italy and Japan – has led inevitably to war. This came with the *blitzkrieg* – literally 'lightning war' – invasion of Poland last September.

The colony is once again a fortress rather than a city, a base for Allied operations in the Mediterranean while invasion by German troops is now a daily threat.

The peninsula's role as an offensive base has been boosted by expansion of the airfield and the forming of Force H, a powerful fleet of 17 British Royal Navy ships including the aircraft carrier *Ark Royal*. This air and sea power gives Britain not only control of the Strait but also extra support for military actions across the Mediterranean Sea.

Engineers have bored into the Rock itself to expand Gibraltar's tunnel network, creating space for new defences and accommodation for the garrison. Material from the tunnelling efforts is being utilised in the development of the airfield, atop the site of the horse-racing track. Gibraltar's tunnels and caves have been the site of human habitation for millennia, but creature comforts now include Nissen huts to stop the constant drip of water, while St Michael's Cave has been transformed into the world's most unusual hospital, complete with pillar-like stalactites. Further plans include a two-lane road tunnel from east to west through the Rock.

Families who have been on the Rock for centuries have left unsure if they will ever return, but their sacrifice ensures the Rock can be a mighty bastion against Nazi aggression.

ES MEDITERRANEAN ERUPTS WITH AXIS

NNELS ARE TRANSFORMED FOR WAR EFFORT

Torch lit for North Africa campaign

THE LONG-AWAITED INVASION OF North Africa, Operation Torch, began today as Allied forces left Gibraltar to wrestle control of the region from the Axis, reports our war correspondent on 8 November 1942.

The first objectives, Morocco and Algeria, are French territories but, with the occupation of mainland France by German troops, their loyalties are uncertain. Allied commanders expect the 100,000 French soldiers and sailors in North Africa either to offer little resistance to their old allies or to join the Free French to fight on their side. Planning for the invasion began last year with the delaying of an invasion to liberate Europe. The Allies insist smashing the Axis' hold on North Africa will allow Italy to be invaded from the south.

Gibraltar's proximity to Africa makes it essential to the success of the operation and Allied forces have been massing in the colony. General Dwight D. Eisenhower, Supreme Commander of the Allied Expeditionary Force, has set up his offices inside the Rock to oversee the operation directly. Over 400 aircraft are available to protect the invasion fleet as it crosses the Strait between Europe and Africa. Two days ago, Gibraltar's powerful fleet, Force H, was dispatched to support the 100,000 British, American and Free French soldiers who began their landings late last night.

The Allied cause has seen many dark days from the Fall of France just two years ago to the destruction of the American fleet at Pearl Harbor and the loss of many key locations in Asia and the Pacific. But the success of Torch would offer a new hope for the Allies, that they might at last see the 'hinge of fate' swing in their favour.

SIKORKSI CRASHES OVER ROCK

IN A SHOCKING TRAGEDY, POLISH Prime Minister and general Władisław Sikorksi has been killed alongside his daughter and eight other passengers, *reports our war correspondent on 4 July 1943*, after his plane crashed into the Mediterranean Sea on take-off from Gibraltar.

The prime minister had been en route to London after visiting Polish troops fighting in the Middle East, stopping off in Gibraltar only briefly. But just 16 seconds after taking off again to continue the journey to London, his plane had crashed. Remarkably, the pilot survived and reported that the steering locked almost immediately after take-off. The unexpected incident has already led some to suspect sabotage may be involved, although the tragic crash seems most likely an accident.

Churchill's concern for Gib's macaques

GIB'S MONKEY TROOP now has 49 members, it was reported today, just six years after then-Prime Minister Winston Churchill intervened after the monkeys nearly died out, writes our environment correspondent on 30 October 1952.

At the start of WW2 the Barbary apes – actually tailless macaque monkeys probably introduced by the Moors or British – were down to just seven individuals. Churchill ordered that five more be brought from North Africa and later took time off from overseeing the Battle of Arnhem to command that, 'the establishment of the monkeys on Gibraltar should be twenty-four, and every effort should be made to reach this number as soon as possible'.

While the survival of the monkeys may appear a minor issue, their presence is associated with British rule of the Rock and is key to the morale of the soldiers stationed at the vital strategic outpost. It is said the monkeys have helped the garrison several times, including during the Great Siege, when they raised the alarm during a night attack.

CELEBRATIONS AS QUEEN ELIZABETH II VISITS GIBRALTAR

BY OUR ROYAL CORRESPONDENT
10 May 1954

THRONGS OF CHEERING Gibraltarians greeted Queen Elizabeth II today as she paid the Rock an official visit. The celebrations took place against a backdrop of growing Spanish hostility which has become increasingly serious over the previous months. Spain is politically opposed to the Queen's visit, which it believes is a deliberate provocation and intended to reinforce Britain's claim to governance over Gibraltar, which Spain has disputed. The Spanish government went as far as to say they could not guarantee Her Majesty's safety during the visit.

None of this was apparent as the Queen arrived at Gibraltar's harbour this morning aboard the Royal Yacht Britannia, along with her husband Prince Philip and their children, Charles and Anne. As they stepped ashore, Governor Sir Gordon Macmillan presented the Queen with the keys to the city before she moved on to an inspection of servicemen at the airfield.

The Queen declared that the 'good government and safe-keeping of the colony and the fortress of Gibraltar' would continue to progress into the future, and paid homage to the Rock's fame 'for its inviolable strength, for the loyalty of its people and for the strategic part it has played on so many different occasions'.

Following last year's coronation, the visit was the final leg of a 12-month tour of the Commonwealth, which while much diminished from the British Empire of just a few years ago, still saw Her Majesty travel around the globe from Jamaica to Australia, Malta and Kenya.

Spanish opposition to the visit includes restrictions on Spanish workers, essential to Gibraltar's economy, crossing the frontier as well as banning Spaniards from taking new jobs on the Rock and preventing import of some goods. It is expected Spain's restrictive measures will continue to grow under dictator Franco, who has made clear his desire to see the Rock become part of Spain again.

However, today's visit shows that Britain's commitment to Gibraltar is as strong as ever – residents of the Rock have held out against Spanish aggression many times before, and will do so again.

GIBRALTAR TV GOES ON AIR

GIBRALTAR TELEVISION made its first broadcast today, writes our culture editor on 7 October 1962. The station, a commercial franchise won by Independent Television Gibraltar, will offer locally produced programmes as well as shows from Britain and the rest of the world. It joins the existing radio service from the Gibraltar Broadcasting Corporation launched just four years ago.

The evening television broadcasts from the new studios in the Wellington Front fortifications are proving an extremely popular addition to the Spanish television available in the area. The radio service runs from morning to midnight with programmes in both English and Spanish.

CABLE CAR OFFERS ROUTE UP ROCK IN RECORD TIME

BY OUR CULTURE EDITOR
1 April 1966

THE SPECTACULAR VIEWS from the Rock of Gibraltar can now be reached by brand-new cable cars entering service today. Thousands of visitors, travelling to Gibraltar en route to other Mediterranean destinations, will now be whisked straight to the viewing platform on its second highest peak, rather than being faced with the daunting climb.

The twin cable cars take visitors 412m up the Rock in just eight minutes to the refurbished remains of the historic Signal Hill Battery.

The location offers fantastic views west over to the Bay, east to the Mediterranean and south to Africa, one of the finest vistas between the two continents. The service also offers easy access to the Apes Den, favourite home of Gibraltar's most mischievous residents. Visitors can return by cable car, or take in Gibraltar's unique landscape on a brisk walk down the Rock.

Inspiration for the cable car came to MH Bland Chairman John G Gaggero on a skiing trip in the Alps, and the network has been built by Swiss cable-car experts Von Roll Holding.

REFERENDUM REAFFIRMS BRITISH RULE
BUT UN AND SPAIN REFUSE TO RECOGNISE RESULTS

95 PER CENT OF GIB'S voters today voted in favour of retaining British rule, *writes our political correspondent on 10 September 1967*. However, the vote has enraged Spain, which insists Gibraltar must be returned to it.

The referendum isn't recognised by the United Nations or Spain, which argues the Rock is a colony that should be handed back to its rightful owners as part of worldwide decolonisation. A Gibraltarian delegation to the UN, led by Chief Minister Sir Joshua Hassan and Leader of the Opposition Peter Isola, offered the view of local people to the UN – that Gibraltarians themselves

wished to retain their close connection with Britain. Their appeals were ignored, but British Minister Judith Hart announced that no transfer of power would take place without a referendum.

The vote follows a petition to the Queen organised by Mrs Angela Smith and Mrs Mariola Summerfield and signed by 96 per cent of Gibraltar's female voters pleading for the Rock to stay British.

Gibraltar's residents have found their movements curtailed by Spanish sanctions including closing the frontier to vehicles and their airspace to planes, forcing pilots to make a dangerous turn against strong winds to land at the airfield.

Gib announces new constitution

A NEW CONSTITUTION for Gibraltar was announced today following the decisive referendum last year, in which Gibraltarians reaffirmed their determination to remain British, writes our political editor on 3 May 1968.

In it, Gibraltar will no longer be a colony but a permanent part of Britain, and its people British rather than just Commonwealth citizens. The new constitution will guarantee self-government, shedding the last vestiges of military governorship. It will also make it law that Britain can't change the sovereignty of Gibraltarians without their consent.

CHAOS AS FRANCO CLOSES FRONTIER
GIBRALTAR LOSES LABOUR FORCE AS FAMILIES TORN APART

BY OUR POLITICAL EDITOR
8 June 1969

HOSTILITIES WITH SPAIN escalated dramatically last night as Franco ordered the total closure of the frontier with Gibraltar, a measure that will drastically affect the daily lives of residents living on either side.

Spanish dictator General Francisco Franco ordered the closure and, with the suspension of the ferry to the Spanish city of Algeciras across the bay planned to take place within the next few days, residents on both sides are utterly cut off. Most tragically, families have been separated, unable to visit each other across the frontier. Telephone and postal communication has also been cut and Gibraltar is once again isolated at the southern end of the Iberian Peninsula.

Spain earlier this month cancelled the work permits of the several thousand impoverished Spaniards who travelled daily to jobs on the Rock. Already, services in Gibraltar have begun to suffer with the Spanish workforce who now, across the border, are struggling to feed their families after losing their jobs. Gibraltarian businesses are looking to Morocco to fill the vacancies and to supply the Rock with crucial goods and services, including oxygen for the hospital and fresh fruit and vegetables.

The harsh measures follow the adoption of Gibraltar's new constitution in May this year, which guarantees the right of Gibraltarians themselves to determine whether the Rock stays British or returns to Spain. This is unacceptable to Spain, which sees the return of the Rock to its sovereignty as a matter of national pride. It is not yet clear how long the frontier will be closed for, but Gibraltarians are preparing for serious disruption to their lives in the days, months and possibly years to come.

Violence breaks out by frontier as 3 shot dead

THREE PROVISIONAL IRA volunteers have been shot dead by plain-clothes soldiers on a Gibraltar street, shocking residents, reports our political correspondent on 6 March 1988.

British intelligence services had information the IRA team drove into Gibraltar today to bomb a military parade. As soldiers from Britain's SAS followed the IRA members, two men and one woman, on foot, they believed they had been spotted and opened fire to prevent the bomb being detonated by remote control.

While the group's car was suspected to contain the bomb, it proved to be empty. However, the search for a second vehicle and the bomb continues.

LENNON AND ONO MARRIED IN GIB

BY OUR CELEBRITIES EDITOR
10 March 1969

BEATLES SUPERSTAR John Lennon and artist Yoko Ono were married in Gibraltar today. Lennon said the pair chose Gibraltar because it was 'quiet, British and friendly'.

After being unable to marry at sea as originally intended, the couple arrived in Gibraltar this morning aboard a private jet, aware the city offered marriages at short notice to British citizens. The two exchanged vows at the Rock Hotel before being officially wed in the Registrars' Office in a 10-minute ceremony. They flew back to Paris an hour later. Lennon is understood to be writing a song about the wedding, in which Gibraltar is described as 'near Spain', words likely to enrage Franco across the frontier.

Lennon is one of the four members of the Beatles, claimed by many to be the greatest rock and pop band ever. Fans fear his marriage will contribute to the break-up of the group following many highly public disputes, some about Ono's growing influence over Lennon's work.

Lennon and Ono are planning a 'bed-in for peace' for their honeymoon – staying in bed for a week as a protest against violence across the globe including the Vietnam War.